The Cold War

American history, Volume 5

Michael Johnson

Published by Harmony House Publishing, 2024.

THE COLD WAR

First edition. March 29, 2024.

Copyright © 2024 Michael Johnson.

ISBN: 979-8224575916

Written by Michael Johnson.

Table of Contents

"To all those who lived through the chill of the Cold War, and to the generations who inherit its legacy, this book is dedicated. May we learn from the trials and triumphs of this tumultuous era, forging a path towards a world of peace and understanding. Let us remember the sacrifices made, the battles fought, and the lessons learned, as we navigate the complexities of our shared global landscape. This dedication is a tribute to resilience, courage, and the enduring quest for a better tomorrow."

Chapter 1: Setting the Stage

The aftermath of World War II witnessed a seismic shift in the geopolitical landscape, as the once-dominant European powers lay in ruins, and two emerging superpowers, the United States and the Soviet Union, rose to prominence. This chapter delves into the complex dynamics that defined the post-war world, exploring the roots of tension between the US and the USSR and setting the stage for the Cold War confrontation.

Introduction to the Geopolitical Landscape Post-World War II

The end of World War II marked the beginning of a new era characterized by uncertainty and reconstruction. Europe, devastated by years of conflict, faced the monumental task of rebuilding its cities, economies, and societies. The United States emerged from the war relatively unscathed, its industrial capacity intact and its economy booming. In contrast, the Soviet Union, though victorious, had suffered immense losses in human lives and infrastructure.

The Allied powers, which had joined forces to defeat the Axis powers, found themselves divided along ideological lines as the post-war settlement took shape. The United States, with its commitment to democracy, free markets, and individual freedoms, stood in stark contrast to the Soviet Union, which espoused communism, centralized planning, and state control. This ideological divergence would form the basis of the rivalry that defined the Cold War.

Emergence of the United States and the Soviet Union as Superpowers

The war had transformed the United States and the Soviet Union into superpowers, endowed with immense military, economic, and political influence on the global stage. The United States, buoyed by its status as the world's largest economy and its possession of nuclear weapons, emerged as the leader of the Western bloc. Its vision of a world order based on liberal democratic principles resonated with many nations seeking stability and prosperity in the post-war era.

Meanwhile, the Soviet Union, under the leadership of Joseph Stalin, consolidated its control over Eastern Europe and sought to spread communism to other parts of the world. The Red Army's advance across Eastern Europe in the final stages of the war established Soviet dominance in the region, setting the stage for the establishment of communist governments loyal to Moscow.

Tensions Brewing Between the Two Nations

Despite their wartime alliance against a common enemy, tensions between the United States and the Soviet Union began to surface even before the guns fell silent. The Yalta and Potsdam conferences, where the leaders of the Allied powers met to discuss the post-war order, highlighted the differences in their respective visions for Europe.

One source of tension was the issue of post-war reconstruction and the division of Germany. While the Allies agreed to divide Germany into four occupation zones, with the Soviet Union, the United States, Britain, and France each administering one zone, disagreements soon arose over the terms of Germany's surrender and the nature of its post-war government.

Another flashpoint was the question of Eastern Europe's future. The Soviet Union, having liberated Eastern European countries from Nazi occupation, sought to establish friendly governments sympathetic to its communist ideology. However, the United States and its Western allies viewed this as an encroachment on the sovereignty of these nations and a violation of the principles of self-determination.

The culmination of these tensions came with the onset of the Cold War, a period of geopolitical rivalry, ideological confrontation, and military build-up between the United States and the Soviet Union. While the two superpowers never engaged in direct military conflict, their competition played out on multiple fronts, shaping the course of world history for decades to come.

As the stage was set for the Cold War to unfold, the world braced itself for a new era of uncertainty and instability, where the specter of nuclear annihilation loomed large and the fate of nations hung in the balance.

Chapter 2: Origins of Conflict

In the aftermath of World War II, the ideological chasm between capitalism and communism widened, laying the groundwork for the Cold War confrontation between the United States and the Soviet Union. This chapter delves into the roots of the conflict, tracing the ideological, diplomatic, and geopolitical factors that fueled tensions between the two superpowers.

Examination of Ideological Differences Between Capitalism and Communism

At the heart of the Cold War lay the fundamental clash between two diametrically opposed ideologies: capitalism and communism. Capitalism, championed by the United States and its Western allies, extolled the virtues of free markets, private property, and individual liberty. Under capitalism, the means of production were privately owned, and economic activity was driven by competition and profit motive.

In contrast, communism, as envisioned by Karl Marx and Friedrich Engels, advocated for the abolition of private property and the establishment of a classless society where the means of production were owned collectively by the state or the community. Under communism, economic planning replaced market forces, and resources were allocated according to the principle of "from each according to his ability, to each according to his needs."

The ideological rivalry between capitalism and communism permeated every aspect of the Cold War conflict, shaping foreign policy decisions, military strategies, and propaganda campaigns on both sides. Each system viewed the other as an existential threat to its way of life, leading to a zero-sum mindset that fueled competition and confrontation.

Seeds of Discord Planted During World War II Conferences

The seeds of the Cold War were sown during the wartime conferences where the Allied powers met to plan the post-war order. The Yalta Conference, held in February 1945, brought together Soviet Premier Joseph Stalin, British Prime Minister Winston Churchill, and US President Franklin D. Roosevelt to discuss the division of Europe and the defeat of Nazi Germany.

At Yalta, tensions simmered beneath the surface as the Allied leaders grappled with competing interests and visions for the future. One key point of contention was the fate of Eastern Europe, which had been liberated by the Red Army and now lay under Soviet influence. Stalin sought to establish friendly governments in the region to serve as a buffer against future aggression, while Churchill and Roosevelt expressed concerns about Soviet expansionism and the erosion of national sovereignty.

The Yalta Conference also laid the groundwork for the division of Germany and the establishment of the United Nations, which was intended to serve as a forum for resolving international disputes and promoting collective security. However, disagreements over the structure and scope of the UN, particularly the composition of the Security Council and the issue of veto power, foreshadowed future diplomatic tensions between the superpowers.

The subsequent Potsdam Conference, held in July-August 1945, further strained relations between the Allies as the realities of post-war Europe began to crystallize. By this time, President Roosevelt had been succeeded by Harry S. Truman, who took a more confrontational stance toward the Soviet Union. The conference saw heated debates over the demarcation of occupation zones in Germany, the punishment of war criminals, and the reconstruction of Europe.

The Breakdown of Wartime Alliances

Despite their wartime alliance against Nazi Germany, the United States and the Soviet Union found themselves increasingly at odds in the immediate aftermath of World War II. The rapid disintegration of the Grand Alliance that had brought them together highlighted the divergent interests and ideologies that would define the Cold War era.

One of the first signs of the breakdown in relations was the refusal of the Soviet Union to withdraw its forces from Eastern Europe after the end of hostilities. Instead, Stalin moved to consolidate Soviet control over the region, installing puppet governments loyal to Moscow and suppressing opposition movements.

In response, the United States and its Western allies grew increasingly wary of Soviet intentions and began to adopt containment as a guiding principle of their foreign policy. Coined by diplomat George F. Kennan in his famous "Long Telegram" from Moscow in 1946, containment sought to prevent the spread of communism beyond its existing borders through a combination of military deterrence, economic aid, and ideological persuasion.

The stage was now set for a new era of conflict and competition, as the United States and the Soviet Union jockeyed for position on the global stage. The Cold War had begun, ushering in a period of uncertainty and instability that would shape the course of world history for the next five decades.

Chapter 3: The Truman Doctrine and Containment

President Harry S. Truman's administration marked a significant turning point in United States foreign policy with the introduction of the Truman Doctrine and the policy of containment. This chapter explores the evolution of these strategies, their impact on the Cold War, and their legacy in shaping the post-war world order.

President Truman's Policy of Containment

As the Cold War intensified in the aftermath of World War II, President Harry S. Truman faced mounting pressure to confront the perceived threat posed by the Soviet Union and its expansionist ambitions. In a speech before a joint session of Congress on March 12, 1947, Truman articulated what would come to be known as the Truman Doctrine, outlining a new approach to US foreign policy aimed at containing the spread of communism.

The Truman Doctrine was a direct response to events unfolding in Greece and Turkey, where communist insurgents threatened to overthrow the established governments and establish pro-Soviet regimes. Truman framed the conflict as a struggle between the forces of democracy and totalitarianism, declaring that it was the duty of the United States to support free peoples resisting attempted subjugation by armed minorities or by outside pressures.

The doctrine represented a departure from the traditional isolationist tendencies of US foreign policy and signaled a willingness to intervene militarily and economically in defense of American interests abroad. Truman justified this interventionism as essential for safeguarding the security and stability of the Western world in the face of Soviet aggression.

Truman's policy of containment laid the groundwork for a series of interventions and alliances aimed at stemming the tide of communism and preserving the balance of power in Europe and Asia. It would become the guiding principle of US foreign policy throughout the Cold War, shaping military strategies, diplomatic initiatives, and aid programs in regions threatened by communist expansion.

Marshall Plan and Aid to War-Torn Europe

Central to Truman's strategy of containment was the economic rehabilitation of war-torn Europe through the implementation of the Marshall Plan. Proposed by Secretary of State George C. Marshall in a speech at Harvard University on June 5, 1947, the plan aimed to provide financial assistance to European countries devastated by World War II, thereby bolstering their economies and fostering political stability.

The Marshall Plan represented a departure from traditional approaches to foreign aid, which had typically been limited in scope and focused on humanitarian relief. Instead, it envisioned a comprehensive program of economic reconstruction that would address the root causes of instability and prevent the spread of communism in Europe.

Under the Marshall Plan, the United States provided over $13 billion (equivalent to approximately $150 billion in today's dollars) in aid to 16 European countries over a four-year period. The funds were used to finance infrastructure projects, modernize industries, and promote trade and investment, laying the foundation for the post-war economic recovery of Western Europe.

The impact of the Marshall Plan was profound, not only in revitalizing the economies of recipient countries but also in strengthening ties between the United States and its European allies. By demonstrating America's commitment to the defense of Western Europe and its willingness to invest in the region's future, the plan helped to cement the transatlantic alliance that would be critical in the Cold War.

Formation of NATO and the Beginnings of the Military Alliance System

In addition to economic aid, Truman sought to bolster Western Europe's security through the formation of a collective defense alliance. The result was the North Atlantic Treaty Organization (NATO), established on April 4, 1949, with the signing of the North Atlantic Treaty by 12 member countries, including the United States, Canada, the United Kingdom, France, and the Benelux countries.

NATO represented a historic commitment to mutual defense and collective security, with member states pledging to come to each other's aid in the event of an armed attack. The treaty's founding principle, articulated in Article 5, stipulated that an attack against one member would be considered an attack against all, triggering a coordinated response.

The creation of NATO marked a significant departure from the traditional balance-of-power politics of the past, where alliances were formed and dissolved based on shifting interests and rivalries. Instead, it represented a long-term commitment to the defense of Western values and institutions against the threat of Soviet expansionism.

The formation of NATO and the implementation of the Truman Doctrine signaled a decisive shift in the Cold War power dynamic, with the United States assuming a leadership role in the defense of the Free World against the communist bloc led by the Soviet Union. It laid the foundation for the military alliance system that would shape the geopolitical landscape for the remainder of the Cold War and beyond.

Impact and Legacy

The Truman Doctrine and the policy of containment had far-reaching implications for US foreign policy, shaping America's approach to global affairs for decades to come. By committing the United States to a strategy of interventionism and collective defense, Truman set a precedent for future administrations to confront perceived threats to American interests and values, even at the risk of military conflict.

The Marshall Plan, meanwhile, demonstrated the power of economic aid as a tool of diplomacy, showing that investment in the prosperity and stability of foreign nations could yield dividends in terms of political allegiance and strategic influence. It laid the groundwork for future development assistance programs and contributed to the emergence of the United States as a global superpower.

Similarly, the formation of NATO established a framework for transatlantic cooperation and military coordination that would prove essential in deterring Soviet aggression and maintaining peace in Europe throughout the Cold War. It solidified the alliance between the United States and its European partners, providing a bulwark against communist expansion and preserving the freedom and security of Western democracies.

In conclusion, the Truman Doctrine and containment represented a paradigm shift in US foreign policy, marking the beginning of an era of active engagement and leadership in global affairs. Through a combination of economic assistance, military alliances, and ideological solidarity, Truman sought to confront the threat of communism and defend the principles of democracy and freedom against totalitarian aggression. Though the Cold War would continue to evolve and escalate in the years that followed, the foundations laid by Truman's policies would endure, shaping the course of world history for generations to come.

Chapter 4: The Berlin Blockade and Airlift

The Berlin Blockade and Airlift stand as one of the defining moments of the early Cold War, showcasing the clash between the United States and the Soviet Union over the future of post-war Europe. This chapter explores the origins, events, and ramifications of the Berlin crisis, highlighting its symbolic significance in shaping Cold War rhetoric and strategies.

Soviet Blockade of West Berlin

In the immediate aftermath of World War II, Berlin, the former capital of Nazi Germany, became a focal point of contention between the Allied powers. Despite being located deep within the Soviet occupation zone of Germany, the city was divided into four sectors, each administered by one of the victorious Allied powers: the United States, the Soviet Union, Britain, and France.

Tensions between the Western Allies and the Soviet Union came to a head in June 1948 when the United States, Britain, and France announced plans to introduce a new currency, the Deutsche Mark, in their respective sectors of Berlin. The move was intended to stabilize the economy of West Germany and pave the way for its integration into the Western bloc.

In response, the Soviet Union, under the leadership of Joseph Stalin, imposed a blockade on all land and water routes leading to West Berlin, effectively cutting off the city from the outside world. The blockade was a brazen attempt to force the Western powers to abandon their plans for currency reform and relinquish control of West Berlin to the Soviet Union.

The blockade of West Berlin presented a grave challenge to the United States and its allies, who now faced the prospect of abandoning the city to Soviet control or risking open conflict with the communist superpower. It also posed a humanitarian crisis for the residents of West Berlin, who were left without access to essential supplies such as food, fuel, and medicine.

The United States Response Through the Berlin Airlift

Faced with the Soviet blockade, President Harry S. Truman and his advisors quickly devised a bold and innovative plan to supply West Berlin by air. Operation Vittles, later renamed the Berlin Airlift, involved a massive airlift operation to transport supplies into the besieged city, circumventing Soviet restrictions on ground and water transportation.

Beginning on June 26, 1948, cargo planes from the United States, Britain, France, and other Western allies began flying round-the-clock missions to deliver food, fuel, and other necessities to West Berlin. The operation required the coordination of hundreds of aircraft, pilots, and ground crews, as well as the construction of new airports and logistical infrastructure.

Despite the logistical challenges and the threat of Soviet interference, the Berlin Airlift proved remarkably successful, delivering an average of 5,000 tons of supplies per day to the people of West Berlin. The operation continued for 15 months, until the Soviet Union finally lifted the blockade on May 12, 1949, in the face of mounting international pressure and the realization that the blockade had failed to achieve its objectives.

The Berlin Airlift was not only a remarkable feat of logistics and cooperation but also a powerful symbol of Western resolve and solidarity in the face of Soviet aggression. It demonstrated the United States' commitment to defending the freedom and security of its allies, even at great cost and risk, and underscored the importance of Berlin as a bastion of democracy in the heart of communist-controlled Eastern Europe.

Symbolism and Significance of the Berlin Crisis in Cold War Rhetoric

The Berlin crisis and the subsequent airlift became a central theme in Cold War rhetoric, symbolizing the broader struggle between democracy and communism for the hearts and minds of the world. For the United States and its allies, West Berlin represented a beacon of freedom and democracy surrounded by the darkness of Soviet tyranny, a living testament to the failure of communism to suppress the human spirit.

Conversely, for the Soviet Union and its allies, the blockade of West Berlin was a calculated display of strength and resolve, intended to demonstrate the superiority of the communist system and its ability to challenge Western hegemony. However, the failure of the blockade and the success of the airlift dealt a significant blow to Soviet prestige and exposed the limitations of Stalin's aggressive tactics.

The Berlin crisis also had far-reaching implications for the future of the Cold War, shaping perceptions of the United States as a global leader and emboldening Western resistance to Soviet expansionism. It reinforced the importance of alliances such as NATO and highlighted the strategic significance of Berlin as a geopolitical flashpoint in the struggle for control of Europe.

In conclusion, the Berlin Blockade and Airlift represented a pivotal moment in the early Cold War, testing the resolve of the United States and its allies in the face of Soviet aggression. The successful defense of West Berlin against the Soviet blockade not only bolstered Western confidence but also set the stage for future confrontations and alliances in the struggle for supremacy between the Free World and the communist bloc.

Chapter 5: The Korean War

The Korean War stands as one of the defining conflicts of the early Cold War period, pitting the forces of communism against those of democracy in a bloody struggle for control of the Korean peninsula. This chapter delves into the origins, course, and consequences of the Korean War, exploring the dynamics of communist expansion, American intervention, and the eventual stalemate that led to the division of Korea.

Communist Expansion into Korea

In the aftermath of World War II, Korea, which had been under Japanese occupation since 1910, found itself divided along the 38th parallel into two separate zones of influence: the Soviet-backed Democratic People's Republic of Korea (North Korea) and the US-backed Republic of Korea (South Korea). The division was intended to be temporary, with the goal of reunifying the country under a single government, but tensions between the two Koreas soon escalated into open conflict.

On June 25, 1950, North Korean forces, under the leadership of Kim Il-sung and with the support of the Soviet Union and China, launched a surprise invasion of South Korea, crossing the 38th parallel and capturing the capital city of Seoul. The attack caught the United States and its allies off guard and threatened to tip the balance of power in Asia in favor of communism.

The North Korean invasion of South Korea marked the beginning of a brutal and protracted conflict that would engulf the Korean peninsula and draw in major powers from around the world. It also served as a catalyst for the United States to reaffirm its commitment to containing communist aggression and defending its allies in the region.

American Intervention and the United Nations Response

In response to the North Korean invasion, the United States, under the leadership of President Harry S. Truman, swiftly intervened to defend South Korea and prevent the spread of communism in Asia. Truman authorized the deployment of American troops to Korea and called for the United Nations Security Council to take action to repel the aggression.

The Security Council, with the Soviet Union absent from the proceedings due to a boycott over the recognition of Taiwan, passed a resolution condemning the North Korean invasion and calling for member states to contribute to a United Nations Command to restore peace and security in Korea. A coalition of 16 countries, led by the United States, contributed troops and resources to the effort, marking the first collective military action undertaken by the UN.

The American-led intervention in Korea was characterized by a combination of conventional warfare, air strikes, and naval blockade aimed at repelling North Korean forces and restoring the status quo ante. Despite initial setbacks and heavy casualties, UN forces, buoyed by reinforcements and superior firepower, succeeded in pushing North Korean troops back across the 38th parallel and liberating South Korean territory.

Stalemate and Division of Korea

The tide of the Korean War shifted dramatically in late 1950 with the entry of Chinese Communist forces into the conflict, in support of their North Korean allies. The intervention of Chinese troops, numbering in the hundreds of thousands, caught UN forces by surprise and pushed them back across the 38th parallel, resulting in a series of bloody battles and high casualties on both sides.

The Korean War soon descended into a grueling war of attrition, with neither side able to achieve a decisive victory or gain significant territorial advantage. The conflict settled into a stalemate along the 38th parallel, with both sides digging in and fortifying their positions in anticipation of a negotiated settlement.

In July 1953, after three years of brutal fighting and failed peace talks, an armistice agreement was signed, effectively bringing an end to the active phase of the Korean War. The agreement established a demilitarized zone (DMZ) along the 38th parallel, with a ceasefire line running through the center, and provided for the exchange of prisoners of war and the establishment of a mechanism for monitoring compliance with the terms of the armistice.

The Korean War left a lasting legacy on the Korean peninsula, as well as on the broader dynamics of the Cold War. Korea remained divided along the 38th parallel, with the North governed by a totalitarian regime under Kim Il-sung and the South emerging as a vibrant democracy and economic powerhouse. The war also solidified US military presence in the region and heightened tensions between the United States and its communist adversaries, setting the stage for future confrontations in Asia and beyond.

In conclusion, the Korean War represented a critical moment in the early Cold War period, showcasing the dangers of communist expansionism and the willingness of the United States to intervene militarily to defend its allies and uphold the principles of democracy and freedom. Though the conflict ended in a stalemate and the division of Korea, its impact on the region and the world would be felt for decades to come.

Chapter 6: McCarthyism and the Red Scare

The era of McCarthyism and the Red Scare stands as a dark chapter in American history, characterized by widespread fear, suspicion, and paranoia over the perceived threat of communist infiltration. This chapter delves into the rise of Senator Joseph McCarthy and his anti-communist crusade, the impact of McCarthyism on American society and politics, and the consequences of the Red Scare for civil liberties and democratic norms.

Senator Joseph McCarthy's Anti-Communist Crusade

The origins of McCarthyism can be traced back to the late 1940s and early 1950s, a time of heightened tensions between the United States and the Soviet Union and growing fears of communist subversion at home. Against this backdrop, Senator Joseph McCarthy, a little-known Republican from Wisconsin, rose to prominence with his relentless attacks on alleged communist sympathizers in government, the media, and academia.

McCarthy first gained national attention in February 1950 when he delivered a speech in Wheeling, West Virginia, in which he claimed to possess a list of 205 known communists working in the State Department. Though McCarthy later revised the number downward and never produced any concrete evidence to support his accusations, the speech catapulted him into the spotlight and set the stage for his anti-communist crusade.

Emboldened by his newfound fame, McCarthy launched a series of highly publicized investigations and hearings aimed at rooting out supposed communist influence in government and society. Operating under the auspices of the Senate Permanent Subcommittee on

Investigations, which he chaired, McCarthy employed aggressive tactics, including intimidation, character assassination, and guilt by association, to target his perceived enemies.

McCarthy's methods were characterized by a lack of due process and a disregard for civil liberties, as he sought to exploit public fears and capitalize on the climate of hysteria surrounding the Red Scare. His reckless accusations and unfounded allegations destroyed careers, ruined lives, and tarnished the reputations of innocent individuals, while also undermining the foundations of democracy and the rule of law.

Impact on American Society and Politics

The impact of McCarthyism on American society and politics was profound and far-reaching, leaving a legacy of fear, suspicion, and division that would endure for decades. At the height of the Red Scare, millions of Americans lived in constant fear of being labeled as communist sympathizers or "fellow travelers" and subjected to scrutiny and persecution by government authorities and private citizens alike.

The climate of fear and paranoia created by McCarthyism led to a wave of loyalty oaths, background checks, and witch hunts targeting suspected subversives in government, academia, and the entertainment industry. Individuals deemed disloyal or un-American were blacklisted from employment, ostracized from society, and subjected to surveillance by the FBI and other law enforcement agencies.

The media played a crucial role in perpetuating the hysteria of McCarthyism, with newspapers, radio programs, and newsreels amplifying the senator's accusations and sensationalizing the threat of communist infiltration. Hollywood, in particular, came under intense scrutiny, as the House Un-American Activities Committee (HUAC) launched investigations into alleged communist influence in the film industry and imposed censorship and self-censorship on artists and filmmakers.

The political fallout from McCarthyism was equally significant, as the fear of being labeled as soft on communism or sympathetic to the Soviet Union led to a climate of conformity and suppression of dissent within both major political parties. Democrats and Republicans alike vied to demonstrate their anti-communist credentials, often at the expense of civil liberties and democratic principles.

Fear of Communist Infiltration and Its Consequences

The fear of communist infiltration and its consequences permeated every aspect of American life during the McCarthy era, shaping public discourse, influencing government policy, and stifling dissent. The specter of Soviet espionage and subversion fueled a frenzy of anti-communist hysteria, as Americans were bombarded with propaganda warning of the dangers posed by communist ideology and its adherents.

The consequences of McCarthyism were felt not only in the realm of politics and government but also in the broader culture and society. Artists, intellectuals, and activists who dared to challenge the prevailing orthodoxy of anti-communism were marginalized, vilified, and subjected to harassment and persecution by government authorities and vigilante groups.

One of the most notorious manifestations of McCarthyism was the phenomenon of McCarthyite witch hunts, in which individuals suspected of communist sympathies or associations were subjected to public scrutiny, interrogation, and persecution. The mere accusation of disloyalty was often enough to ruin a person's career, destroy their reputation, and cast a shadow of suspicion over their entire life.

The legacy of McCarthyism continues to resonate in American society and politics to this day, serving as a cautionary tale of the dangers of political extremism, demagoguery, and the erosion of civil liberties in the name of national security. The Red Scare of the 1950s serves as a stark reminder of the fragility of democracy and the importance of safeguarding the principles of free speech, due process, and the rule of law in the face of threats real and imagined.

In conclusion, McCarthyism and the Red Scare represented a dark chapter in American history, characterized by fear, paranoia, and persecution in the name of anti-communism. The rise of Senator Joseph McCarthy and his crusade against alleged subversives left a lasting impact on American society and politics, undermining trust in government institutions, dividing the nation along ideological lines, and chilling dissent and free expression for years to come.

Chapter 7: The Space Race

The Space Race of the mid-20th century stands as a defining chapter in the history of the Cold War, symbolizing the competition between the United States and the Soviet Union for supremacy in science, technology, and ideological influence. This chapter explores the origins, milestones, and consequences of the Space Race, focusing on Soviet successes with Sputnik and Yuri Gagarin, the American response through the Apollo program, and the broader implications of space exploration as a battleground for ideological supremacy.

Soviet Successes with Sputnik and Yuri Gagarin

The Space Race officially began on October 4, 1957, when the Soviet Union launched Sputnik 1, the world's first artificial satellite, into orbit around the Earth. The launch of Sputnik took the world by surprise and served as a wake-up call to the United States, which had long held a technological edge over its Cold War rival.

Sputnik's success was a propaganda coup for the Soviet Union, demonstrating the capabilities of Soviet science and technology and challenging American claims of superiority. The tiny satellite, equipped with a radio transmitter that emitted a simple "beep" signal, orbited the Earth for 21 days before its batteries died, but its impact on global consciousness was profound.

Just four years later, on April 12, 1961, the Soviet Union scored another triumph in the Space Race with the launch of Vostok 1, carrying cosmonaut Yuri Gagarin, the first human to travel into space and orbit the Earth. Gagarin's historic flight captured the imagination of people around the world and cemented the Soviet Union's reputation as a leader in space exploration.

Gagarin's successful mission marked a significant milestone in the Space Race, demonstrating the feasibility of manned spaceflight and raising the stakes for the United States in the quest to catch up with its Cold War adversary. It also served as a potent symbol of Soviet technological prowess and ideological superiority, fueling fears in the United States of falling behind in the arms race and losing the battle for hearts and minds in the developing world.

American Response and the Apollo Program

In response to the Soviet Union's early successes in space, the United States embarked on an ambitious program to regain the initiative and assert its leadership in space exploration. Central to this effort was the Apollo program, a series of manned lunar missions aimed at landing American astronauts on the moon and returning them safely to Earth.

The Apollo program was launched in 1961 by President John F. Kennedy, who set the ambitious goal of landing a man on the moon before the end of the decade as a demonstration of American technological prowess and resolve. Kennedy's famous speech at Rice University in 1962, in which he declared, "We choose to go to the moon," galvanized public support for the space program and provided the impetus for NASA to push the boundaries of human exploration.

The Apollo program proceeded in stages, with a series of unmanned test flights and manned missions designed to test the capabilities of the spacecraft and prepare for the eventual lunar landing. After several setbacks and tragedies, including the loss of Apollo 1 astronauts in a launch pad fire in 1967, NASA achieved its goal on July 20, 1969, when Apollo 11 astronauts Neil Armstrong and Buzz Aldrin became the first humans to set foot on the moon.

The success of the Apollo 11 mission was a triumph of American ingenuity, determination, and teamwork, and it captured the imagination of people around the world. Armstrong's iconic words, "That's one small step for man, one giant leap for mankind," echoed the sentiments of millions who watched in awe as humanity reached out to touch the stars.

Space Exploration as a Battleground for Ideological Supremacy

The Space Race was about more than just scientific achievement or national prestige; it was also a battleground for ideological supremacy between the United States and the Soviet Union. Both superpowers saw space exploration as a means of demonstrating the superiority of their respective political and economic systems and winning the hearts and minds of people around the world.

For the Soviet Union, the success of Sputnik and Yuri Gagarin's historic flight served as a powerful propaganda tool, showcasing the benefits of socialism and communism and undermining American claims of technological superiority. Soviet leaders hailed their achievements in space as evidence of the superiority of the socialist system and the inevitability of its triumph over capitalism.

For the United States, the Space Race represented an opportunity to demonstrate the virtues of democracy, freedom, and free enterprise on a global stage. American leaders portrayed the Apollo program as a triumph of human ingenuity and American exceptionalism, showcasing the spirit of innovation and entrepreneurship that defined the American way of life.

The competition between the United States and the Soviet Union in space also had geopolitical implications, as both superpowers sought to establish strategic footholds in orbit and project power beyond the Earth's atmosphere. The development of intercontinental ballistic missiles (ICBMs) and reconnaissance satellites gave both sides the ability to monitor each other's activities and potentially launch nuclear weapons from space, heightening tensions and raising the stakes in the Cold War.

In conclusion, the Space Race was a defining feature of the Cold War era, shaping the course of history and influencing the trajectory of human civilization. From the launch of Sputnik to the Apollo moon landings, the competition between the United States and the Soviet Union in space pushed the boundaries of human achievement and demonstrated the power of science and technology to shape the future of humanity. While the Space Race may have ended with the collapse of the Soviet Union and the conclusion of the Apollo program, its legacy lives on in the collective memory of mankind and the ongoing exploration of the cosmos.

Chapter 8: Cuban Missile Crisis

The Cuban Missile Crisis of October 1962 stands as one of the most perilous moments of the Cold War, bringing the world to the brink of nuclear war and threatening the very existence of humanity. This chapter explores the background to the crisis, including the Bay of Pigs invasion and the Cuban Revolution, the discovery of Soviet missiles in Cuba, and the negotiations and brinkmanship between President John F. Kennedy and Soviet Premier Nikita Khrushchev that ultimately averted catastrophe.

Background to the Crisis: Bay of Pigs Invasion and Cuban Revolution

The roots of the Cuban Missile Crisis can be traced back to the early 1960s, a time of intense rivalry and conflict between the United States and the Soviet Union. In January 1959, Fidel Castro and his revolutionary forces overthrew the American-backed regime of Fulgencio Batista, establishing a communist government in Cuba and aligning the island nation with the Soviet bloc.

The rise of Castro and the spread of communism in the Western Hemisphere sent shockwaves through the United States, which viewed Cuba as a strategic threat and a potential beachhead for Soviet expansionism in the Americas. In April 1961, President John F. Kennedy authorized the ill-fated Bay of Pigs invasion, a CIA-backed operation aimed at overthrowing Castro and toppling his regime.

The Bay of Pigs invasion, launched by a force of Cuban exiles trained and equipped by the United States, ended in disaster, with the invaders quickly defeated and captured by Castro's forces. The botched operation not only embarrassed the Kennedy administration but also solidified Castro's grip on power and pushed Cuba further into the Soviet orbit.

Discovery of Soviet Missiles in Cuba

In the aftermath of the Bay of Pigs fiasco, Castro and the Soviet Union grew increasingly wary of American attempts to undermine their revolution and remove them from power. Seeking to deter future aggression and protect their strategic interests in the Western Hemisphere, Soviet Premier Nikita Khrushchev and Castro reached a secret agreement to deploy nuclear missiles to Cuba.

Beginning in the summer of 1962, Soviet ships began transporting intermediate-range ballistic missiles (IRBMs) and nuclear warheads to Cuba, hidden beneath decks of cargo and concealed from American surveillance. The deployment of Soviet missiles to Cuba caught the United States off guard and set off alarm bells in Washington, D.C., as intelligence agencies scrambled to assess the threat and formulate a response.

On October 14, 1962, American U-2 reconnaissance planes flying over Cuba spotted the telltale signs of Soviet missile installations, including launch pads, support facilities, and nuclear warheads. The discovery of Soviet missiles in Cuba sent shockwaves through the Kennedy administration and triggered a frantic scramble to devise a strategy for confronting the Soviet Union and averting a nuclear showdown.

Negotiations and Brinkmanship Between Kennedy and Khrushchev

Faced with the prospect of nuclear war, President Kennedy and his advisors grappled with how best to respond to the Soviet missile threat in Cuba. After considering various options, including military strikes and a naval blockade, Kennedy opted for a combination of diplomacy and coercion, seeking to compel Khrushchev to remove the missiles through a combination of carrot and stick.

On October 22, 1962, President Kennedy addressed the nation in a televised speech, announcing the discovery of Soviet missiles in Cuba and imposing a naval quarantine, or blockade, around the island to prevent further shipments of weapons and supplies. Kennedy demanded that Khrushchev remove the missiles and dismantle the launch sites, warning of dire consequences if his demands were not met.

The world held its breath as the United States and the Soviet Union engaged in a high-stakes game of brinkmanship, with both sides teetering on the edge of nuclear catastrophe. Tensions mounted as American ships enforced the blockade and Soviet ships steamed toward Cuba, threatening to breach the quarantine and escalate the crisis to the brink of war.

Behind the scenes, Kennedy and Khrushchev engaged in a flurry of diplomatic exchanges and back-channel negotiations, seeking to defuse the crisis and find a face-saving solution for both sides. Through a series of letters and secret communications, the two leaders explored possible avenues for resolving the standoff and preventing a nuclear exchange.

The turning point in the crisis came on October 27, 1962, when Khrushchev offered to withdraw Soviet missiles from Cuba in exchange for a public pledge from the United States not to invade the island and a private commitment to remove American Jupiter missiles from Turkey. Kennedy accepted Khrushchev's offer, defusing the crisis and averting a nuclear catastrophe.

On October 28, 1962, Khrushchev announced the Soviet Union's decision to remove its missiles from Cuba, bringing an end to the Cuban Missile Crisis and restoring a semblance of calm to the world. The crisis had lasted for 13 tense days, during which the fate of humanity hung in the balance and the specter of nuclear war loomed large over the globe.

Consequences and Legacy

The Cuban Missile Crisis had far-reaching consequences for the United States, the Soviet Union, and the world at large. For the United States, the crisis exposed vulnerabilities in American intelligence and military capabilities and underscored the dangers of brinkmanship and escalation in the nuclear age. It also prompted a reassessment of US policy toward Cuba and the Soviet Union, leading to a period of détente and arms control negotiations in the years that followed.

For the Soviet Union, the Cuban Missile Crisis marked a humiliating retreat and a setback for Khrushchev's leadership, as the removal of Soviet missiles from Cuba was seen as a capitulation to American pressure. The crisis also strained relations between the Soviet Union and Cuba, as Castro felt betrayed by Khrushchev's decision to withdraw the missiles without consulting him.

For the world at large, the Cuban Missile Crisis served as a wake-up call to the dangers of nuclear proliferation and the perils of superpower confrontation. It highlighted the need for dialogue, diplomacy, and arms control measures to prevent future crises and reduce the risk of nuclear war.

In conclusion, the Cuban Missile Crisis of October 1962 was a pivotal moment in the history of the Cold War, testing the resolve of the United States and the Soviet Union and bringing the world to the brink of nuclear annihilation. Through a combination of diplomacy, coercion, and brinkmanship, President Kennedy and Premier Khrushchev managed to defuse the crisis and avert disaster, but the legacy of those harrowing days continues to resonate in the collective memory of mankind as a stark reminder of the fragility of peace and the dangers of nuclear weapons.

Chapter 9: Vietnam War

The Vietnam War stands as one of the most contentious and divisive conflicts in modern history, shaping the course of American foreign policy and leaving a profound legacy of trauma and disillusionment. This chapter explores the origins of the Vietnam War, including the communist insurgency in Vietnam, American involvement, and the escalation of conflict, as well as the lasting impact of the war on American foreign policy and society.

Communist Insurgency in Vietnam

The roots of the Vietnam War can be traced back to the struggle for independence and self-determination in Vietnam, which had been under French colonial rule for much of the 19th and 20th centuries. In the aftermath of World War II, Vietnamese nationalist forces, led by Ho Chi Minh and the Viet Minh, launched a guerrilla campaign against French colonial authorities, seeking to liberate their country from foreign domination.

The First Indochina War, fought between the Viet Minh and the French colonial forces from 1946 to 1954, ended in victory for the Vietnamese insurgents and the withdrawal of French troops from Vietnam. The Geneva Accords of 1954 divided Vietnam along the 17th parallel, with Ho Chi Minh's communist forces controlling the north and a pro-Western regime, backed by the United States, governing the south.

Despite the division of Vietnam, tensions between the communist north and the anti-communist south continued to simmer, fueled by ideological differences, territorial disputes, and the legacy of colonialism. In the late 1950s, communist insurgents in the south, known as the Viet Cong, launched a campaign of guerrilla warfare and sabotage aimed at overthrowing the South Vietnamese government and reunifying the country under communist rule.

The Viet Cong insurgency posed a serious threat to the stability of South Vietnam and its American backers, who viewed the conflict through the lens of the Cold War and the global struggle against communism. As the insurgency intensified, the United States became increasingly involved in Vietnam, providing military aid, advisors, and financial assistance to the South Vietnamese government in its fight against the communists.

American Involvement and Escalation of Conflict

American involvement in Vietnam escalated significantly under President Lyndon B. Johnson, who inherited the conflict from his predecessor, John F. Kennedy, and made the Vietnam War a central focus of his administration's foreign policy. In August 1964, following alleged attacks on American warships in the Gulf of Tonkin, Congress passed the Gulf of Tonkin Resolution, granting Johnson broad authority to escalate US military involvement in Vietnam.

The Gulf of Tonkin Resolution marked the beginning of a massive escalation of American military presence in Vietnam, as US forces were deployed in ever-increasing numbers to combat the Viet Cong insurgency and support the South Vietnamese government. The US military conducted large-scale bombing campaigns, launched search-and-destroy missions, and engaged in counterinsurgency operations aimed at rooting out communist guerrillas and their supporters.

Despite the influx of American troops and resources, the Vietnam War quickly devolved into a quagmire, with no clear end in sight and mounting casualties on both sides. The conflict took a heavy toll on the Vietnamese people, with widespread destruction, displacement, and loss of life, as well as on American soldiers, who faced guerrilla warfare, jungle conditions, and a determined enemy.

The Tet Offensive of January 1968, in which the Viet Cong launched coordinated attacks on cities and military installations across South Vietnam, marked a turning point in the Vietnam War and shattered the myth of American invincibility. Though the offensive was ultimately repelled by US and South Vietnamese forces, it dealt a severe blow to American morale and raised doubts about the viability of the war effort.

Legacy and Impact of the Vietnam War on American Foreign Policy

The Vietnam War had a profound and far-reaching impact on American foreign policy, shaping attitudes toward military intervention, foreign aid, and the use of force in the post-Cold War era. The war shattered the myth of American exceptionalism and exposed the limits of US power and influence in the face of determined nationalist movements and guerrilla warfare.

The Vietnam War also sparked a crisis of confidence in American institutions and leadership, as the government's credibility was called into question and public trust in elected officials eroded. The war fueled social unrest and anti-war protests at home, as millions of Americans took to the streets to demand an end to the conflict and the withdrawal of US troops from Vietnam.

The Vietnam War also had a lasting impact on American society and culture, giving rise to a generation of disillusioned veterans and anti-war activists who questioned the morality and wisdom of American interventionism abroad. The war became a symbol of American hubris and folly, a cautionary tale of the dangers of military adventurism and the human cost of war.

In conclusion, the Vietnam War was a watershed moment in American history, shaping the course of foreign policy and national identity for decades to come. The conflict exposed the limits of American power and influence in the post-Cold War era and left a legacy of trauma and disillusionment that continues to resonate in the collective memory of the nation. Despite its tragic and divisive nature, the Vietnam War remains a crucial chapter in the ongoing quest for understanding and reconciliation in American society.

Chapter 10: Détente

Détente, a French term meaning "relaxation," refers to a period of easing Cold War tensions between the United States and the Soviet Union during the 1970s. This chapter explores the thawing of Cold War tensions under President Richard Nixon and Soviet Premier Leonid Brezhnev, focusing on key initiatives such as the Strategic Arms Limitation Talks (SALT) and the Helsinki Accords, as well as the broader implications of détente for international relations and human rights diplomacy.

Thawing of Cold War Tensions under Nixon and Brezhnev

The seeds of détente were sown in the late 1960s, as both the United States and the Soviet Union sought to deescalate Cold War tensions and find common ground on issues of mutual concern. President Richard Nixon, who took office in January 1969, made improving relations with the Soviet Union a central goal of his administration, seeking to achieve a more stable and predictable relationship with America's superpower rival.

Nixon's approach to détente was based on the principles of realpolitik, or practical politics, emphasizing the pursuit of pragmatic and mutually beneficial agreements with the Soviet Union, rather than ideological confrontation or military brinkmanship. Nixon believed that by engaging with the Soviets in areas of mutual interest, such as arms control and trade, it would be possible to reduce the risk of conflict and promote greater stability in international relations.

Soviet Premier Leonid Brezhnev, for his part, also saw value in pursuing détente with the United States, recognizing the benefits of reducing Cold War tensions and improving relations with the world's leading superpower. Brezhnev, who came to power in 1964 following the ouster of Nikita Khrushchev, sought to consolidate his leadership and strengthen the Soviet Union's position on the world stage through diplomacy and detente.

The thawing of Cold War tensions under Nixon and Brezhnev was marked by a series of high-level meetings and diplomatic exchanges aimed at building trust and fostering cooperation between the two superpowers. These included the signing of agreements on arms control, trade, and cultural exchange, as well as symbolic gestures of goodwill, such as state visits and summit meetings between Nixon and Brezhnev.

Strategic Arms Limitation Talks (SALT)

One of the key initiatives of détente was the Strategic Arms Limitation Talks (SALT), a series of negotiations between the United States and the Soviet Union aimed at limiting the growth of their nuclear arsenals and reducing the risk of nuclear war. The first round of SALT talks, known as SALT I, took place between 1969 and 1972, culminating in the signing of the Anti-Ballistic Missile (ABM) Treaty and the Interim Agreement on the Limitation of Strategic Offensive Arms in May 1972.

The ABM Treaty, which was ratified by both the United States and the Soviet Union, limited the deployment of anti-ballistic missile systems designed to intercept incoming nuclear missiles, thereby reducing the risk of a destabilizing arms race in missile defense technology. The Interim Agreement, meanwhile, placed temporary limits on the number of intercontinental ballistic missiles (ICBMs) and submarine-launched ballistic missiles (SLBMs) that each side could deploy, as well as restrictions on the development of new weapons systems.

The SALT I agreements represented a significant breakthrough in arms control and disarmament efforts, marking the first time that the United States and the Soviet Union had agreed to impose limits on their nuclear arsenals. While the agreements did not eliminate the threat of nuclear war altogether, they helped to reduce tensions and build confidence between the two superpowers, laying the groundwork for future arms control negotiations.

The Helsinki Accords and Human Rights Diplomacy

Another milestone of détente was the signing of the Helsinki Accords in August 1975, a comprehensive agreement aimed at promoting security, cooperation, and human rights in Europe. The accords, which were signed by 35 countries, including the United States, the Soviet Union, and the countries of Western and Eastern Europe, were the result of a series of negotiations that took place over two years, culminating in a summit meeting in Helsinki, Finland.

The Helsinki Accords consisted of three main "baskets" or sections: security, cooperation, and human rights. The security basket included commitments to respect the territorial integrity and sovereignty of all participating states, refrain from the threat or use of force, and resolve disputes peacefully through negotiation and dialogue.

The cooperation basket focused on enhancing economic, scientific, cultural, and environmental cooperation among the signatory states, with the goal of promoting mutual understanding and goodwill between East and West.

The human rights basket, perhaps the most controversial aspect of the Helsinki Accords, affirmed the importance of respecting and protecting fundamental human rights and freedoms, including freedom of speech, religion, and movement. While the Soviet Union initially sought to downplay the significance of the human rights provisions, viewing them as a concession to the West, the accords ultimately helped to shine a spotlight on human rights abuses in Eastern Europe and provided a platform for dissident voices to be heard.

The Helsinki Accords represented a significant achievement in international diplomacy, offering a framework for peaceful coexistence and cooperation between East and West and laying the groundwork for future efforts to promote democracy, human rights, and the rule of law. While the accords did not bring about an immediate end to the Cold War or resolve all of the underlying tensions between the United States and the Soviet Union, they helped to create a more stable and predictable environment for international relations in Europe and beyond.

Legacy and Impact of Détente

The legacy of détente is a complex and multifaceted one, with both positive and negative consequences for international relations and global security. On the one hand, détente helped to reduce Cold War tensions and promote greater stability and predictability in relations between the United States and the Soviet Union. The arms control agreements negotiated under détente, such as SALT I, laid the groundwork for future efforts to limit the proliferation of nuclear weapons and reduce the risk of nuclear war.

Détente also opened up new avenues for dialogue and cooperation between East and West, fostering cultural exchange, scientific collaboration, and economic interdependence between the two superpowers. The signing of the Helsinki Accords, in particular, helped to promote human rights and democracy in Eastern Europe and provided a framework for addressing longstanding grievances and promoting greater openness and transparency in international relations.

On the other hand, détente was not without its critics, who viewed the policy as a form of appeasement or capitulation to the Soviet Union and accused the United States of sacrificing its principles and values in the pursuit of short-term diplomatic gains. Critics also pointed to continued Soviet aggression and expansionism in regions such as Afghanistan and Africa as evidence that détente had failed to fundamentally alter the nature of the Cold War or moderate Soviet behavior.

In conclusion, détente represents a complex and nuanced chapter in the history of the Cold War, characterized by both cooperation and competition between the United States and the Soviet Union. While détente helped to reduce tensions and promote greater stability and predictability in relations between the two superpowers, its legacy remains a subject of debate and interpretation, with differing perspectives on its effectiveness and long-term impact on global security and diplomacy.

Chapter 11: Proxy Wars

Proxy wars, often termed as "wars by proxy" or "proxy conflicts," are conflicts where two opposing countries support combatants that serve their interests instead of waging war directly against each other. These wars are characterized by superpower involvement, regional instability, and the use of local actors as proxies to advance geopolitical agendas. This chapter delves into notable proxy wars during the Cold War era, including conflicts in Afghanistan, Angola, and Nicaragua, examining superpower involvement, tactics, and strategies employed by both sides.

Conflicts in Afghanistan, Angola, and Nicaragua

1. Afghanistan: The Soviet invasion of Afghanistan in December 1979 marked the beginning of one of the most significant proxy wars of the Cold War era. The Soviet Union intervened in Afghanistan to prop up the communist government of the Democratic Republic of Afghanistan, which was facing a growing insurgency by Islamist mujahideen fighters. The United States, along with its allies in the Muslim world, including Saudi Arabia and Pakistan, provided support to the mujahideen, supplying weapons, training, and funding to the anti-communist guerrillas. The conflict, which lasted until 1989, resulted in a bloody stalemate and had far-reaching consequences for Afghanistan, contributing to the rise of radical Islamist groups and laying the groundwork for future conflicts in the region.

2. Angola: The civil war in Angola, which began in 1975 following the country's independence from Portugal, quickly became a proxy battleground for Cold War rivals. The Soviet Union and Cuba supported the leftist People's Movement for the Liberation of Angola (MPLA), which came to power following independence, while the United States and South Africa backed the National Front for the Liberation of Angola

(FNLA) and the National Union for the Total Independence of Angola (UNITA), both of which were anti-communist and anti-MPLA. The conflict, which lasted until 2002, resulted in widespread devastation and loss of life, with millions of Angolans displaced and tens of thousands killed in the fighting.

3. Nicaragua: The Nicaraguan civil war, which erupted in the late 1970s following the overthrow of the Somoza dictatorship, became another proxy battleground for Cold War rivals. The Sandinista National Liberation Front (FSLN), a leftist revolutionary movement, seized power in Nicaragua in 1979, leading to a violent insurgency by the Contras, a counter-revolutionary group supported by the United States. The Reagan administration provided military and financial support to the Contras, known as the "Contra aid," as part of its efforts to roll back communist influence in Central America. The conflict, which lasted until the early 1990s, resulted in widespread human rights abuses and political instability in Nicaragua, as well as strained relations between the United States and its Latin American neighbors.

Superpower Involvement in Regional Conflicts

Superpower involvement in regional conflicts during the Cold War was driven by a desire to advance geopolitical interests, contain the spread of communism, and gain strategic advantage over rival powers. Both the United States and the Soviet Union sought to exploit local conflicts to further their own agendas, often at the expense of the countries and peoples caught in the crossfire.

In Afghanistan, for example, the Soviet Union intervened to prop up the communist government and maintain a strategic foothold in the region, while the United States supported the mujahideen fighters as part of its efforts to bleed the Soviets and undermine their control over Central Asia.

In Angola, the Soviet Union and Cuba supported the MPLA government to expand communist influence in Southern Africa, while the United States and South Africa backed the anti-communist factions to prevent the spread of socialism and maintain Western dominance in the region.

In Nicaragua, the United States supported the Contras to overthrow the Sandinista government and prevent the establishment of a communist regime in Central America, while the Soviet Union provided limited support to the Sandinistas to challenge American hegemony in the Western Hemisphere.

Tactics and Strategies Used by Both Sides

Proxy wars during the Cold War era were characterized by a variety of tactics and strategies employed by both superpowers and their proxies to gain the upper hand in regional conflicts.

1. Arms and Equipment: Both the United States and the Soviet Union supplied their respective proxies with weapons, ammunition, and military equipment to strengthen their capabilities and undermine their adversaries. This included small arms, artillery, tanks, aircraft, and other military hardware, as well as training and logistical support to maintain and operate these weapons effectively.

2. Propaganda and Psychological Warfare: Propaganda and psychological warfare were important tools used by both sides to influence public opinion, sow discord among enemy ranks, and bolster support for their own cause. This included leaflet drops, radio broadcasts, and other forms of communication aimed at spreading disinformation, demoralizing the enemy, and rallying support for the proxy forces.

3. Guerrilla Warfare and Insurgency: Many proxy conflicts during the Cold War era were fought using guerrilla warfare tactics, including hit-and-run attacks, ambushes, sabotage, and terrorism. These tactics allowed weaker, irregular forces to harass and weaken their better-equipped adversaries, while also avoiding direct confrontation and minimizing casualties.

4. Foreign Intervention and Support: Foreign intervention and support played a crucial role in shaping the outcome of proxy conflicts, with both superpowers and their allies providing military, financial, and logistical assistance to their proxies to gain strategic advantage and achieve their objectives. This often involved covert operations, clandestine funding, and arms shipments to bolster the capabilities of local insurgent groups and undermine their adversaries.

In conclusion, proxy wars were a defining feature of the Cold War era, characterized by superpower rivalry, regional instability, and the use of local actors as proxies to advance geopolitical agendas. Conflicts in Afghanistan, Angola, and Nicaragua, among others, served as battlegrounds for Cold War rivalries, with devastating consequences for the countries and peoples caught in the crossfire. Despite efforts to contain the spread of communism and maintain strategic advantage, proxy wars often proved costly, unpredictable, and ultimately unsustainable, underscoring the limitations of military force and the complexities of international relations in the post-World War II era.

Chapter 12: Reagan and the Second Cold War

The presidency of Ronald Reagan, spanning from 1981 to 1989, marked a significant shift in US foreign policy towards the Soviet Union and ushered in a period of renewed confrontation and tension, often termed as the "Second Cold War." This chapter explores Ronald Reagan's confrontational approach to the Soviet Union, his implementation of the Strategic Defense Initiative (SDI), and the economic pressures that contributed to the collapse of the Soviet Union.

Ronald Reagan's Confrontational Approach to the Soviet Union

Ronald Reagan entered office in January 1981 with a deeply-held belief in the need to confront and contain Soviet expansionism and communism. He viewed the Soviet Union as an "evil empire" that posed a grave threat to freedom, democracy, and US interests around the world. Reagan's confrontational approach to the Soviet Union was informed by a staunch anti-communist ideology and a commitment to rolling back Soviet influence wherever it existed.

Reagan's foreign policy towards the Soviet Union was characterized by a combination of military buildup, economic pressure, and ideological warfare. He sought to challenge Soviet power and prestige on multiple fronts, including support for anti-communist movements, increased defense spending, and aggressive rhetoric aimed at undermining the legitimacy of the Soviet regime.

Reagan's confrontational stance towards the Soviet Union was evident in his support for anti-communist rebels in Afghanistan, Nicaragua, and other hotspots around the world. He provided military and financial assistance to anti-Soviet guerrilla groups, such as the mujahideen in Afghanistan and the Contras in Nicaragua, as part of his efforts to undermine Soviet influence and roll back communist gains.

Reagan's confrontational approach to the Soviet Union also extended to arms control negotiations and diplomatic relations. While he expressed a willingness to engage in dialogue with Soviet leaders, including General Secretary Mikhail Gorbachev, Reagan remained committed to maintaining a strong military deterrent and pursuing policies that put pressure on the Soviet Union to change its behavior.

Strategic Defense Initiative (SDI) and the Arms Race

One of the key pillars of Reagan's confrontational approach to the Soviet Union was the Strategic Defense Initiative (SDI), a proposed missile defense system aimed at protecting the United States from nuclear attack. Reagan announced the SDI program in a televised address to the nation on March 23, 1983, describing it as a "vision of the future" and a means of rendering nuclear weapons "impotent and obsolete."

The SDI program, also known as "Star Wars," envisioned a network of ground-based and space-based missile interceptors capable of shooting down incoming enemy missiles before they reached their targets. The goal of the SDI program was to create a defensive shield that would make nuclear weapons "impotent and obsolete," thereby reducing the risk of nuclear war and increasing US security.

The announcement of the SDI program sent shockwaves through the Soviet leadership, who viewed it as a direct threat to their strategic nuclear deterrent and a potential game-changer in the arms race. The Soviet Union responded by ramping up its own military spending and research efforts, leading to a renewed escalation of the arms race and heightened tensions between the superpowers.

While the SDI program ultimately failed to live up to its ambitious goals and was criticized for its technical feasibility and cost, it nonetheless had a significant impact on US-Soviet relations and the broader dynamics of the Cold War. The SDI program served as a catalyst for increased military spending and technological innovation, fueling fears of a new arms race and raising concerns about the possibility of a destabilizing nuclear arms race in space.

Economic Pressures and the Collapse of the Soviet Union

In addition to military and diplomatic pressures, Reagan's confrontational approach to the Soviet Union also relied on economic pressures to weaken the Soviet economy and hasten the collapse of the Soviet Union. Reagan believed that by imposing economic sanctions, trade restrictions, and other measures, the United States could undermine the Soviet Union's ability to sustain its military buildup and support for communist regimes around the world.

One of the key elements of Reagan's economic strategy towards the Soviet Union was the use of trade restrictions and economic sanctions to limit Soviet access to Western technology, capital, and markets. Reagan imposed restrictions on high-technology exports to the Soviet Union, including computer technology, telecommunications equipment, and advanced manufacturing technology, in an effort to deny the Soviet Union access to critical resources and hinder its economic development.

Reagan also sought to exploit vulnerabilities in the Soviet economy by targeting key sectors, such as energy and agriculture, where the Soviet Union was heavily dependent on imports from the West. By restricting access to these essential goods and resources, Reagan hoped to increase pressure on the Soviet leadership and force them to reconsider their aggressive foreign policy and military buildup.

The economic pressures exerted by Reagan's policies, combined with internal economic problems and political unrest within the Soviet Union, contributed to a mounting crisis of legitimacy and confidence in the Soviet system. As the Soviet economy faltered and public discontent grew, Soviet leaders were forced to confront the reality of their declining power and influence on the world stage.

In conclusion, Ronald Reagan's confrontational approach to the Soviet Union during the 1980s ushered in a period of renewed tension and conflict, often referred to as the "Second Cold War." Reagan's confrontational stance towards the Soviet Union, coupled with his implementation of the Strategic Defense Initiative (SDI) and economic pressures, contributed to a renewed escalation of the arms race and heightened tensions between the superpowers. While Reagan's policies were controversial and divisive, they ultimately played a significant role in hastening the collapse of the Soviet Union and bringing an end to the Cold War.

Chapter 13: Perestroika and Glasnost

The era of Perestroika and Glasnost, under the leadership of Mikhail Gorbachev, represented a radical departure from the rigid and authoritarian policies of previous Soviet leaders. This chapter delves into Gorbachev's reforms and attempts to modernize the Soviet Union, the impact of Perestroika and Glasnost on Eastern Europe and satellite states, and the unintended consequences that ultimately led to the dissolution of the Soviet Union.

Gorbachev's Reforms and Attempts to Modernize the Soviet Union

Mikhail Gorbachev assumed leadership of the Soviet Union in March 1985, facing a daunting array of economic, political, and social challenges. Determined to revitalize the stagnant Soviet economy and address widespread public discontent, Gorbachev embarked on a bold program of reform known as Perestroika, or "restructuring," and Glasnost, or "openness."

Perestroika aimed to modernize and decentralize the Soviet economy, introducing elements of market competition, private enterprise, and economic restructuring to stimulate growth and innovation. Gorbachev sought to break free from the rigid central planning model of the Soviet economy, which had led to inefficiency, stagnation, and widespread shortages of consumer goods.

Under Perestroika, Gorbachev introduced a series of economic reforms aimed at promoting enterprise autonomy, encouraging foreign investment, and streamlining bureaucratic inefficiencies. These included measures such as allowing limited private ownership of businesses, granting greater decision-making authority to individual enterprises, and liberalizing price controls to reflect market forces.

Glasnost, meanwhile, aimed to promote greater openness and transparency in Soviet society, lifting restrictions on freedom of speech, press, and political dissent. Gorbachev recognized the need to address growing public disillusionment with the Soviet system and the deep-seated problems of corruption, censorship, and repression that had long plagued Soviet society.

Glasnost encouraged public debate, intellectual freedom, and cultural expression, allowing previously taboo topics to be discussed openly and challenging the authority of the Communist Party and state-controlled media. Gorbachev's efforts to promote Glasnost led to a flowering of artistic, literary, and political expression, as well as a reevaluation of Soviet history and ideology.

Impact on Eastern Europe and Satellite States

The impact of Perestroika and Glasnost extended far beyond the borders of the Soviet Union, reverberating throughout Eastern Europe and the satellite states of the Warsaw Pact. Gorbachev's reforms unleashed a wave of political ferment and nationalist fervor in the region, as people sought to break free from Soviet domination and assert their own national identities.

In Eastern Europe, the reforms of Perestroika and Glasnost inspired popular movements for political change and democratic reform, leading to the downfall of communist regimes in countries such as Poland, Hungary, East Germany, Czechoslovakia, and Romania. The collapse of communism in Eastern Europe was driven by a combination of internal pressure from dissident movements and external pressure from Gorbachev's policies of reform and openness.

The fall of the Berlin Wall in November 1989, symbolizing the reunification of East and West Germany, marked a watershed moment in the collapse of communism in Eastern Europe and the end of the Cold War division of Europe. The events of 1989, often referred to as the "Revolution of the Velvet" or the "Autumn of Nations," unleashed a wave of democratic revolutions and popular uprisings across the region, leading to the dismantling of the Iron Curtain and the end of Soviet hegemony in Eastern Europe.

In the Soviet Union's satellite states, the impact of Perestroika and Glasnost was felt most acutely in countries such as Poland, Hungary, and Czechoslovakia, where popular movements for political reform and independence gained momentum in the late 1980s. Gorbachev's decision to pursue a policy of non-intervention and "non-interference" in the internal affairs of Eastern European countries further emboldened pro-democracy activists and hastened the collapse of communist rule.

Unintended Consequences and the Dissolution of the Soviet Union

Despite Gorbachev's intentions to reform and revitalize the Soviet Union, the reforms of Perestroika and Glasnost ultimately had unintended consequences that hastened the collapse of the Soviet system. The loosening of political controls and the erosion of central authority weakened the Communist Party's grip on power, leading to a power vacuum and political paralysis at the highest levels of government.

Economic restructuring under Perestroika exacerbated existing problems of inflation, unemployment, and shortages, as well as creating new challenges of market instability, corruption, and income inequality. The transition from a centrally planned economy to a market-oriented system proved to be a painful and disruptive process, causing widespread dislocation and hardship for millions of ordinary Soviet citizens.

The dismantling of censorship and control over the media led to a flood of information and criticism that undermined public confidence in the Soviet system and exposed the failures and injustices of communist rule. Gorbachev's attempts to promote openness and transparency inadvertently opened the floodgates to a torrent of discontent and dissent that swept away the foundations of Soviet power.

The dissolution of the Soviet Union in December 1991, following a failed coup attempt by hardline communist elements, marked the end of an era and the beginning of a new chapter in world history. The collapse of the Soviet Union was a seismic event that reshaped the geopolitical landscape of Eurasia, bringing an end to the Cold War rivalry between East and West and heralding the emergence of a multipolar world order.

In conclusion, Perestroika and Glasnost represented a bold experiment in reform and renewal that ultimately led to the collapse of the Soviet Union and the end of the Cold War. Gorbachev's attempts to modernize and democratize the Soviet system unleashed forces that he could not control, leading to unintended consequences and the dissolution of the Soviet empire. Despite its failures and shortcomings, Perestroika and Glasnost opened the door to a new era of freedom, democracy, and opportunity for millions of people in the former Soviet Union and Eastern Europe, leaving a lasting legacy of hope and change that continues to shape the world today.

Chapter 14: The End of the Cold War

The end of the Cold War, a decades-long standoff between the United States and the Soviet Union, marked a pivotal moment in world history, reshaping the global geopolitical landscape and ushering in a new era of international relations. This chapter examines the key events leading to the end of the Cold War, including the fall of the Berlin Wall, the dissolution of the Soviet Union, and the assessment of the Cold War's legacy and its implications for the modern world.

Fall of the Berlin Wall

The fall of the Berlin Wall on November 9, 1989, symbolized the collapse of communism in Eastern Europe and the end of the Cold War division of Europe. The Berlin Wall, erected by the East German government in 1961 to stem the flow of refugees fleeing to the West, had become a potent symbol of the division between East and West, a physical barrier separating families, friends, and communities.

The fall of the Berlin Wall was precipitated by a combination of internal and external factors, including popular discontent with communist rule, economic stagnation, and political repression, as well as the policies of reform and openness pursued by Soviet leader Mikhail Gorbachev. Gorbachev's refusal to intervene militarily to prop up the faltering East German regime sent a signal to other Eastern European countries that they were free to pursue their own paths of political reform and democratization.

The fall of the Berlin Wall unleashed a wave of euphoria and jubilation across Europe, as people from both East and West celebrated the reunification of Germany and the end of Soviet domination in Eastern Europe. The events of 1989, often referred to as the "Revolution of the Velvet" or the "Autumn of Nations," set in motion a chain reaction of democratic revolutions and popular uprisings that ultimately led to the collapse of communism in Eastern Europe and the end of the Cold War.

Dissolution of the Soviet Union and the End of the Warsaw Pact

The dissolution of the Soviet Union in December 1991 marked the formal end of the Cold War and the disintegration of one of the world's largest and most powerful empires. The collapse of the Soviet Union was the culmination of years of internal decay, economic stagnation, and political turmoil, exacerbated by Gorbachev's policies of reform and openness.

Gorbachev's attempts to modernize and democratize the Soviet system through Perestroika and Glasnost inadvertently undermined the foundations of Soviet power, weakening the Communist Party's grip on power and exposing the failures and injustices of communist rule. Economic restructuring under Perestroika exacerbated existing problems of inflation, unemployment, and shortages, leading to widespread discontent and social unrest.

The dissolution of the Soviet Union was hastened by a series of political and economic crises, including the failed coup attempt by hardline communist elements in August 1991 and the declaration of independence by the Baltic republics and other Soviet republics. The collapse of the Soviet Union unleashed a wave of nationalist fervor and ethnic conflict, as newly independent states sought to assert their sovereignty and chart their own paths of development.

The end of the Cold War also brought about the dissolution of the Warsaw Pact, the military alliance formed by the Soviet Union and its satellite states in Eastern Europe to counter NATO. With the collapse of communism in Eastern Europe and the withdrawal of Soviet troops, the Warsaw Pact lost its relevance and was formally dissolved in July 1991, signaling the end of the Soviet Union's hegemony in the region.

Assessment of the Cold War's Legacy and its Implications for the Modern World

The end of the Cold War had far-reaching implications for the modern world, reshaping the global geopolitical landscape and ushering in a new era of international relations. The collapse of communism in Eastern Europe and the Soviet Union led to the emergence of a multipolar world order, characterized by the rise of new regional powers and the decline of traditional superpowers.

The end of the Cold War also brought about a period of unprecedented economic globalization and technological innovation, as barriers to trade and communication were dismantled and new opportunities for cooperation and exchange emerged. The spread of democracy and human rights, while uneven and incomplete, gained momentum in the wake of the Cold War, as former communist countries embraced political reform and liberalization.

At the same time, the end of the Cold War also brought about new challenges and threats to global security, including the proliferation of weapons of mass destruction, transnational terrorism, and ethnic conflict. The collapse of communism in Eastern Europe and the Soviet Union unleashed a wave of nationalism and ethnic violence, as newly independent states struggled to forge national identities and resolve long-standing territorial disputes.

In conclusion, the end of the Cold War marked a transformative moment in world history, reshaping the global geopolitical landscape and opening up new opportunities for cooperation and exchange. The collapse of communism in Eastern Europe and the Soviet Union, while bringing about the end of one era, also ushered in a new era of uncertainty and instability, as the world grappled with the challenges and opportunities of a post-Cold War world.

Chapter 15: Lessons Learned

The Cold War, spanning over four decades, had a profound impact on global politics, shaping the course of international relations and influencing the strategies and ideologies of nations around the world. As we reflect on the lessons learned from this tumultuous period in history, we must consider the Cold War's legacy and its relevance in the 21st century, as well as the challenges and opportunities for international relations in a post-Cold War world.

Reflections on the Cold War's Impact on Global Politics

The Cold War fundamentally transformed the global political landscape, dividing the world into two competing blocs led by the United States and the Soviet Union. The rivalry between capitalism and communism, democracy and authoritarianism, defined the ideological contours of international relations and fueled conflicts and proxy wars in regions around the world.

One of the lasting legacies of the Cold War was the proliferation of nuclear weapons and the emergence of the doctrine of mutually assured destruction (MAD), which held that any use of nuclear weapons would result in catastrophic consequences for both sides. The specter of nuclear war cast a long shadow over the Cold War era, shaping military strategies, arms control negotiations, and crisis management efforts.

The Cold War also witnessed the expansion of military alliances, such as NATO and the Warsaw Pact, which served as bulwarks against the perceived threats posed by the opposing superpower bloc. These alliances provided security guarantees to member states and helped to maintain stability and deterrence in Europe and other regions of strategic importance.

At the same time, the Cold War fueled a global arms race, as both the United States and the Soviet Union sought to outmatch each other in terms of military capabilities and technological innovation. The proliferation of conventional and nuclear weapons, as well as the development of ballistic missile systems and other delivery platforms, raised the stakes of confrontation and increased the risk of conflict escalation.

Relevance of Cold War Strategies and Ideologies in the 21st Century

While the Cold War officially ended with the collapse of the Soviet Union in 1991, its legacy continues to reverberate in the 21st century, shaping the strategies and ideologies of nations around the world. The rivalry between great powers, geopolitical competition, and the pursuit of strategic interests remain defining features of international politics, albeit in different forms and contexts.

The resurgence of great power competition, particularly between the United States, China, and Russia, has raised concerns about a new Cold War-like confrontation in the 21st century. Tensions over territorial disputes, military buildups, and ideological differences have fueled speculation about the potential for conflict and instability in key regions of the world, such as the Asia-Pacific and Eastern Europe.

The legacy of the Cold War also continues to influence debates over national security, foreign policy, and the role of military force in addressing global challenges. The doctrine of containment, articulated by George Kennan during the early years of the Cold War, remains relevant today as policymakers grapple with the rise of revisionist powers and the spread of authoritarian regimes.

Ideologically, the contest between democracy and authoritarianism, freedom and oppression, continues to shape the ideological fault lines of international relations. The struggle for human rights, democratic governance, and the rule of law remains a central theme in global politics, as nations seek to balance the imperatives of security and stability with the demands of freedom and justice.

Challenges and Opportunities for International Relations in a Post-Cold War World

The end of the Cold War brought about new challenges and opportunities for international relations, as the world grappled with the complexities of a post-Cold War world. The collapse of communism in Eastern Europe and the Soviet Union created new opportunities for cooperation and integration, as former adversaries sought to build a more peaceful and prosperous future.

At the same time, the end of the Cold War also unleashed new sources of instability and conflict, as old rivalries resurfaced and new threats emerged on the horizon. The proliferation of weapons of mass destruction, the spread of terrorism and extremism, and the rise of non-state actors have posed unprecedented challenges to global security and stability, requiring coordinated and multilateral responses from the international community.

The rise of globalization and technological innovation has transformed the nature of international relations, connecting nations and peoples in ways that were unimaginable during the Cold War era. The advent of the internet, social media, and digital communications has revolutionized the way information is disseminated and power is exercised, creating new opportunities for diplomacy, dialogue, and engagement across borders.

In conclusion, the Cold War was a defining moment in world history, shaping the course of international relations and leaving a lasting legacy that continues to influence global politics to this day. As we reflect on the lessons learned from this tumultuous period, we must recognize the enduring relevance of Cold War strategies and ideologies in the 21st century, while also acknowledging the challenges and opportunities for international relations in a post-Cold War world. By learning from the past and adapting to the realities of the present, we can build a more peaceful, stable, and prosperous future for generations to come.

Don't miss out!

Visit the website below and you can sign up to receive emails whenever Michael Johnson publishes a new book. There's no charge and no obligation.

https://books2read.com/r/B-A-OREFB-NOKAD

BOOKS 2 READ

Connecting independent readers to independent writers.

Did you love *The Cold War*? Then you should read *World War II*[1] by Michael Johnson!

"World War II: America's Role in the Global Conflict" chronicles the pivotal moments that defined America's involvement in the greatest conflict of the 20th century. From the seeds of conflict to the enduring legacy, delve into the chapters that shaped history, from America's initial stance of isolationism to its transformation into a global superpower. Experience the courage and sacrifice of those who fought on the front lines and the resilience of those who endured on the home front. This book is a testament to the indomitable spirit of the American people and their enduring legacy in shaping the world we live in today.

---

1. https://books2read.com/u/3k9aa8

2. https://books2read.com/u/3k9aa8

About the Author

Michael Johnson is a distinguished historian specializing in American history. With a degree in History from Harvard University, Johnson's work delves into pivotal moments, figures, and themes shaping the United States. He has authored numerous acclaimed books, offering insightful perspectives and engaging narratives. Johnson's commitment to meticulous scholarship and compelling storytelling has earned him widespread acclaim in the field. Passionate about sharing his expertise, he frequently engages in lectures and public events to foster a deeper appreciation for America's past.